Why is the Sky Blue?

And Other Nature Questions Kids Ask!

Jem Brooks

Before you start reading...

To let you know how much I appreciate you, dear reader, I have a written another special book for you!

"376 Wacky World Facts Kids Should Know!"

Download it for <u>FREE</u> by going to the link below!

www.horusbooks.com/free

Table of Contents

Why Do You See Lightning Before You Hear Thunder?

When lightning travels from a thundercloud down to the ground, a small "channel" of ionized air is formed between the sky and the ground. When this channel breaks, it makes the sound we call thunder!

Even though you hear thunder after lightning, both the thunder and the lightning are actually formed at the same time! But since sound moves at a slower speed than light, a flash of lightning will be seen before thunder can be heard.

<u>Did you know?</u>
The Earth has 100 lightning strikes per second - 3.6 billion per year!

How is Snow Made?

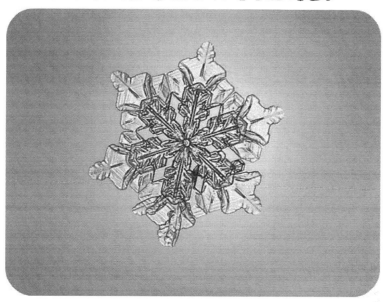

Although a snowy landscape looks beautiful and serene, did you know that it starts with a violent collision? It's true! Tiny ice crystals must first collide against each other in order to form snowflakes up in the clouds. If the weather isn't cold enough, they will melt and turn to sleet or rain when they fall.

It takes a combination of moisture in the air, bits of dirt and very cold air in order to make snow. Water vapor forms ice crystals around tiny bits of dirt that travel in the air. Then the ice crystals get stuck together, and will fall to the earth as snow.

Why Does Quicksand Make You Sink?

Quicksand is not a bottomless pit waiting to suck you down like in the movies!

Actually, quicksand is really just ordinary sand that has a lot of extra water added into it. With so much water, the small sand particles are too separated to be able to stick together. You sink because the sand is simply too mushy for you to gain solid footing and also because it can't support your weight

If you get into quicksand- don't struggle! If you relax, your body will float right back up to the top.

Did you know?
Because quicksand needs a combination of sand and water, you are likely to find quicksand near a river, not a desert!

How Does the Ocean Make Waves?

Ocean waves are caused by wind. Wind blows over the water, and as it hits the water it forms a ripple. The ripple continues to be pushed by the wind and grows bigger until it becomes a large wave.

The speed of the wind can affect how big a wave will be. If the wind is traveling very fast, the wave will be bigger. The amount of time the wind blows will also determine the size of the wave. The longer the wind blows, the bigger the wave will become.

<u>Did you know?</u>
Some waves can travel thousands of miles from their original starting point!

Why Do Leaves Change Color In the Fall?

Plants use a process called "photosynthesis" to feed themselves. During photosynthesis, light helps turn water and carbon dioxide into sugar to feed the plant.

To help photosynthesis work, plants use chlorophyll, which is the green color you see in the leaves. As fall approaches, and plants get less light, they can no longer make sugar and begin live off of stored sugars. Therefore photosynthesis slows and chlorophyll is no longer needed so leaves begin to change from green to brown.

<u>Did you know?</u>
Not all trees lose their leaves in the fall. Conifer trees, such as the pine, spruce, fir, hemlock and cedar stay evergreen year round!

How Did the Continents Form?

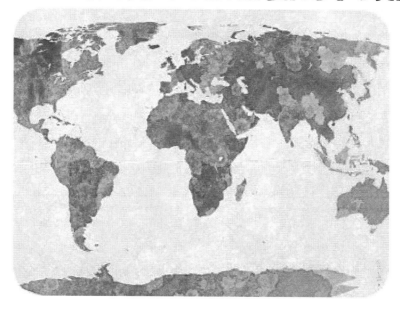

The continents started out with one big, violent crash that occurred over 340 million years! The crash formed a big supercontinent known as "Pangaea" and caused valleys and mountains to form, making Pangaea look like a big puzzle.

Later, the continents began breaking up, a process called "rifting" by geologists. As the continents separated, the water surrounding them began to fill in the gaps. It took about 140 million years for the continents to divide as they are now.

Did you know?
Scientists predict that a new supercontinent will be formed in another 250 million years. The continents are continuing to rift and will eventually crash into each other again, forming the newest supercontinent, named "Pangea Ultima."

What Causes Volcanoes to Erupt?

A volcano is really just a mountain than opens downward into a pool of molten rock, called magma.

The Earth's surface is made up of many plates, and sometimes, when these plates move, they create friction which can cause a volcano to erupt.

As the molten rock erupts from the volcano, it is called "lava."

Did you know?
More than half of the world's volcanoes are located in the Pacific Ocean. They form a circle-like shape and are known as the Ring of Fire.

How Do Tornadoes Form?

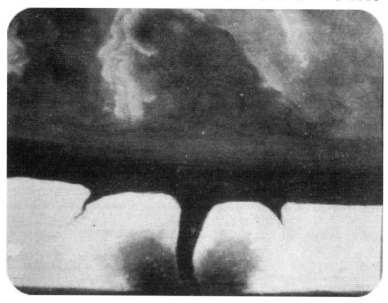

When cool, dry air from Canada and warm, moist air from the Gulf of Mexico meet, the atmosphere becomes very unstable. This causes a lot of warm air to rise quickly and cool air to fall, the perfect atmosphere to form a tornado!

Have you ever watched an ice skater execute a perfect spin? The skater will spin faster and faster as she pulls her hands closer to her spinning body. It is the same with a tornado. As the tornado forms, it begins to spin, stretching upward and rotating faster. The faster the tornado spins, the more powerful it becomes.

Did you know?
You can make your own tornado in a jar! Just fill a old jar about ¾ full of water, a teaspoon of liquid soap a teaspoon of vinegar. Tighten the lid then swirl the jar in a circular motion. The liquid will form a small tornado!

Where Do Diamonds Come From?

Diamonds are actually minerals, and are made up of carbon. They are formed naturally in the earth, just like gold and silver.

They come from deep within the earth, where they are formed under pressure and heat applied for a very long time. It can take from 1 to 3 billion years for a diamond to be ready!

The diamond is considered to be the hardest natural material known to man. Some industries even use diamonds for cutting and polishing tools.

Did you know?
The word "diamond" came from the Greek language, and means "unbreakable."

Why is the Ocean Salty?

The most common mineral in the ocean is salt, which would account for why it tastes so salty! In fact, salt makes up approximately 85% of the mineral content in ocean water!

As the Earth's crust gradually erodes, dissolved minerals from the ground are washed into the sea. Minerals such as sodium, chlorine, sulfur, calcium, magnesium and potassium add to the "saltiness" of the sea water.

When water evaporates from the ocean or freezes to ice, it also leaves behind salt!

Did you know?
The Red Sea is located in the Indian Ocean. It is also known as the "Dead Sea," because its salt content is so high, nothing can stay alive in it!

Why is the Sky Blue?

This is a question that many of the world's most intelligent people have asked for centuries! And yet, the answer is actually very simple. The color of the sky is determined by dust. Yes, that's right-dust!

There are trillions of tiny dust particles in the Earth's atmosphere, and most of these are far too small for us to see. The smallest dust particles in the air are the same length as the wavelengths of blue light. And because blue light bounces from one particle to another, whenever you look at the sky in any direction you see blue light.

Did you know?

On rainy days, moisture droplets reflect all wavelengths equally. This changes the color of the sky, making it look either white or gray.

Why is the Grass Green?

The green color in grass is due to a pigment called Chlorophyll, which is a chemical that helps the grass with a process called "photosynthesis" (something we talked about in a previous question!).

Chlorophyll is essential for helping plants go through photosynthesis so that they can produce food, and that is why most plants are green!

Did you know?

You can make art with chlorophyll! Take a few blades of fresh grass or leaves and put them in between a piece of folded white paper. Rub firmly on the outside of the paper with the edge of a spoon. When you open the paper, the chlorophyll from the plants will have transferred a design onto your paper.

How Much Does the Earth Weigh?

The Earth weighs a whopping 6 sextillion metric tons. You would need a **VERY** big scale to try to weigh the Earth!

What would that look like written out? To make it easy, you start with a 6 and add 21 zeros. Here's what it looks like:
6,000,000,000,000,000,000,000 metric tons.

What's even crazier is that the Earth is gaining weight! Every year it gains about 40,000 metric tons due to receiving extra weight from space debris.

Did you know?
The planet Mars has a lower gravity than planet Earth. Therefore, a person who weighs 200 pounds on Earth would only weigh 76 pounds on Mars!

Why Do We Have Seasons?

Seasons change because the Earth rotates around the sun. The time it takes for the Earth to fully rotate around the Sun is what we consider a full year on our calendar.

At times during the Earth's trip, part of the planet is closer to the Sun. When our part of the Earth is closest to the Sun, we experience the hottest days of summer.

During other times, our part of the planet is further away from the Sun. At this time half of the planet experiences the cold winter.

Did you know?
Because each part of the Earth experiences a different season at the same time of the year, Christmas in Austrailia is not filled with snow, but that sun and sand! Kids get to play in the pool while they wait for Santa!

What Causes Earthquakes?

The Earth isn't made up of one big slab of rock. Instead, it is made up of several large pieces called "plates." The plates fit together much like a giant jigsaw puzzle. But sometimes these plates move and get stuck against each other, creating a large amount of energy.

When the pressure from the energy gets too great, it is release, setting off vibrations or "waves." These are known as earthquakes.

Earthquakes can be rolling, shaking or cause a sudden shock to the earth's surface.

Did you know?

Somewhere in the world, there is an earthquake once every 30 seconds. Some earthquakes are barely felt, while others are much larger and can cause damage.

Why Does Water Stick Together?

Water is made up of molecules that stick together because they are attracted to each other. This attraction is called "cohesion" by scientists. Cohesion helps the water become "sticky" and hold onto other drops of water.

If you look closely at a drop of water on a smooth surface such as a board, you can see that it almost looks as if the drop has a "skin" protecting its shape.

Did you know?

You can demonstrate cohesion for yourself. All you need is a penny and a small bottle of water with a medicine dropper. Add one drop of water at a time on the head of a penny. Watch how the water drops cling together until a dome is formed over the penny. When the amount of water is too much, the dome will eventually break and the water will spill over!

How Deep is the Ocean?

The ocean is so big, it covers approximately 70% of the Earth's surface! The average ocean depth is about 14,000 feet. That's about 2.65 miles straight down!

However, the deepest part of the ocean is in the Mariana Trench, which is about 7 miles deep. Not only is the trench deep, but it is 1,554 miles long and 44 miles wide, making it 120 times larger than the Grand Canyon!

Did you know?
It takes approximately 5 hours to reach the bottom of Mariana Trench using highly sophisticated submarines!

What is the Chance That I Will Get Struck By Lightning?

The odds that a person will get struck by lightning are very slim!

According to the U.S. National Weather Service, the average chance is one in a million. Of course, this number can change depending upon where you live and what precautions you take during a thunderstorm.

The best way to avoid lightning is to go inside immediately when thunderstorms are in your area! The safest place is inside. Stay away from windows and doors, and avoid using phones, computers or other electrical equipment.

<u>Did you know?</u>
The possibility of getting struck twice by lightning is one in 360 billion!

What Causes Wind?

Wind is caused by the Sun warming the surface of the Earth. As the atmosphere warms up, warm air rises and cool air moves in to replace the rising warm air, which creates the movement of the blowing wind.

Short bursts of wind are known as gusts. Soft winds are called breezes, while strong, destructive winds are called hurricanes.

Wind can be used to provide movement for turbines, which create energy to power lights and run machines. Ships use wind to power their sails. Activities like paragliding, kite flying and wind surfing rely on wind.

<u>Did you know?</u>
The planets Neptune and Saturn have the fastest winds in the entire solar system!

Are Monkeys and Humans Related?

Many years ago, a scientist named Charles Darwin wrote that all species have changed over time from their common ancestors. This is called "evolution."

Humans and monkeys are both primates, but humans did not descend from monkeys. Instead, both humans and chimpanzees descended from a common ape ancestor that lived between 6 to 8 billion years ago. Some other animals descended from the same ancestor are orangutans and gorillas.

<u>Did you know?</u>
When humans smile, we interpret it as a gesture of friendship or kindness. However, chimpanzees interpret a smile as baring teeth, and see it as a sign of aggression or danger.

Why Can't I feel the Earth Rotating?

Because the Earth moves at a very slow, constant pace while rotating, you don't notice any movement. Additionally, everything that is on the Earth, including yourself, move along with it, making it very difficult to feel the Earth move.

However, if the Earth were to suddenly stop, speed up, or rotate backwards- then you would notice it for sure!

Ancient people mistakenly thought that the Earth stood still and the stars, Sun and the Moon were physically moving above them!

Did you know?
The Earth spins at 1,000 miles per hour! Even though this seems very fast, it is actually a speed slow enough that you do not notice the Earth is moving!

If I Swallow a Watermelon Seed, Will It Grow In My Stomach?

Watermelon seeds cannot grow in your stomach!

All seeds need moisture, the correct temperature, sunlight, and oxygen to grow. Because it cannot get these things in your stomach, the seed will not germinate.

Additionally, when a watermelon seed is swallowed, it passes into your stomach and is bathed in acids that are designed to break down foods, not help them grow. Seeds will pass through the body and be eventually eliminated.

Did you know?
The heaviest watermelon on record was grown in Arkansas in 2005, and weighed 268.8 pounds!

What is Air Made Out of?

Air is made up of two main elements- nitrogen and oxygen. The largest element is nitrogen, as it makes up 78.05%, while oxygen makes up 20.95%. That leaves 1% which is a blend of argon, carbon dioxide, neon, helium, methane and krypton.

Air also has particles of dust, bacteria, spores and water. The water content in air can be different, depending upon where you live. In the desert, the water content in air can be less than 0.1%. In warmer areas, such as Hawaii, the air can contain over 6% water due to the humidity.

Did you know?
Air covers the Earth in a layer that is over 400 miles high!

How Do Seashells Make An Ocean Sound?

Have you ever put a beautiful shell to your ear and heard the sound of the waves crashing against the shore?

Sadly, seashells do not carry the sound of the ocean inside them.

Instead, they have a lot of hard curved surfaces, which reflect sound. When you put the shell to your ear, what you hear is the echoes bouncing of all the walls inside the shell.

Did you know?
You can produce an "ocean" sound without a seashell. Place an empty cup over your ear. Try moving the cup slowly away from your ear until you hear the ocean!

What Came First, the Chicken or the Egg?

This question is difficult to answer because there are many competing theories on the subject.

However, the most common answer to whether a chicken or egg came first is that both the chicken and the egg came about at the same time!

Another animal that was a non-chicken evolved over time to become an almost-chicken. This animal then laid an egg that hatched into the first true chicken on Earth, and that is how the cycle of chickens and eggs began!

Did you know?
Studies have revealed that eating an egg a day can make you smarter. Who knows, it might even make you an "eggs-pert"!

Why Do Flowers Smell?

Flowers produce a sweet smell in order to attract bees, butterflies and hummingbirds.

Flowers need these insects and birds to help them with the process of "pollination." Pollination is the distribution of pollen from one flower to another. Pollen needs to be transferred like this because it is the only way more flowers can be made.

When the insects and birds visit a flower to use its nectar for food, pollen "hitches a ride" and gets transferred to another flower.

Did you know?

Not all flowers smell so sweet! Some flowers, like the Eastern Skunk Cabbage, are smelly in order to attract flies to help them pollinate, because flies aren't attracted to sweet smells, but they do like stinky, smelly flowers!

Where Do Butterflies Go When It Rains?

When it rains, butterflies hide under large leaves or crawl under rocks to keep dry. Some butterflies will sit in the bushes with their wings tightly held against their bodies.

If they are not in flight, butterflies will rest with their head in a downward position. This is because they like to sit high up on a tree trunk, and can watch what is going on below them. This position also gives their wings the most exposure to the sunlight so they can dry quickly.

Did you know?
Butterflies have a "special sense" when it comes to wet or windy weather. They can sense a change in the weather several hours before it arrives! Butterflies are very sensitive to changes in humidity and air pressure.

Why is the North Pole Cold All Year?

The North Pole is always cold because it is located at the very top point of the Earth. Because it is furthest away from the Sun, it doesn't get as much direct sunlight as the middle part of the Earth. So it stays very, very cold all year long.

Located in the middle of the Arctic Ocean, the North Pole is surrounding by ice. The ice is about 6 to 10 feet thick. The ocean depth at the North Pole is more than 13,123 feet deep. In the winter, the temperature is around minus 29° degrees, and in the summer it warms up to 32° degrees!

Did you know?
The North Pole does not belong to one specific country because it is part of international waters.

How Does Coral Grow?

Coral isn't a plant, it's actually made up of tiny animals called "polyps." The polyps have a hard outer skeleton, kind of like a snail's shell.

The polyps attach to each other to form a colorful ocean community, known as a "coral reef." As more new, young polyps get added to the community, the older polyps lift themselves upward, making way for the new polyps underneath.

Did you know?
Coral has been used in the making of some anti-cancer drugs. Who knew such tiny ocean beings could help save lives?

Why is Lake Water Not Salty?

Lakes are not salty because they get a new source of fresh water from rain. Fresh groundwater also enters the lakes through rivers and rivers leaving the lakes remove water, taking some of the saltiness with it.

There are a few lakes in the world that don't have outlets to get rid of salty groundwater, so the salt content in the water is very high. One of the most famous of these is the Dead Sea. This lake gets its name because nothing can grow in it due to the extreme saltiness.

Did you know?
Salty water helps things float. Fill a clear glass halfway with warm water. Add salt one tablespoon at a time. Each time you add the salt, gently place an egg in the glass to see if it floats. If it doesn't float, remove the egg and add more salt. Try again. Watch as the egg eventually floats in the glass!

What is Global Warming?

Global warming is the gradual increase of temperature in our climate. As the climate gets warmer, changes happen to our world. The Arctic sea ice melts faster, storms and floods become stronger, flowers bloom earlier and birds lay eggs sooner. Some animals, like bears, may even stop hibernating!

Global warming happens because we use fuel sources that release a lot of carbon dioxide into the atmosphere. By using alternative energy sources such as solar energy or wind, we can decrease the amount of carbon dioxide released.

Did you know?
There is more carbon dioxide in the atmosphere today than at any point in the last 800,000 years.

Why Does It Rain So Much in the Rainforest?

Rainforests are located in regions known as the "tropics." The climate in the tropics is rainy and the temperature is warm. The air is humid, due to the combination of rain and sun.

The rainforest gets a lot of rain throughout the year. But what most people don't realize is that the trees in the rainforest also "sweat" water, making it seem like it is raining all the time! Steam also rises from the rainforest floor, adding more moisture to the already wet environment.

Due to the moist environment, rainforests are a great place for plants to grow healthy and strong.

Did you know?
Tropical rainforests make up a large portion of the Earth's oxygen supply!

How Do Animals Become Endangered?

Sometimes changes in the Earth, caused by nature or humans, can affect how an animal species lives.

For example, when an animal's habitat is threatened or removed, it no longer has a place to live and will eventually die.

An entire species can also be killed in the event of a terrible natural disaster, like a volcano eruption, or by humans who hunt the animal for food, clothing, or game.

<u>Did you know?</u>
Years ago, the American crocodile was hunted for its skin. The skin was made into shoes and purses. So many American crocodiles were killed that it is now an endangered species!

Where is the Tallest Place on Earth?

Mt. Everest is the tallest mountain. It is located in the Himalayan mountain range, between Nepal and Tibet.

Standing at 29,035 feet tall, Mt. Everest has the highest elevation in the world! This awe-inspiring wonder draws climbers from every corner of the Earth, daring to climb its dizzying heights.

Many people have tried to scale Mt. Everest, but not all expeditions have been victorious. The first successful climber to reach the summit of Mt. Everest was Edmund Hillary from New Zealand in 1953.

Did you know?
The people of Nepal call Mt. Everest "Sagarmtha" which means "forehead in the sky."

Why is the Earth Round?

The Earth is round because gravity- the force that pulls everything toward the center of the world- affects the shape. Gravity pulls equally on the Earth in every direction.

Even if the Earth had any edges or sharp points sticking out, gravity would pull them back into the center again and smooth them out, keeping the shape nice and round.

Did you know?
When you toss a ball in the air, it comes back toward you, instead of flying off into space. The force of gravity that shapes our world also pulls the ball back to the center of the Earth!

Why Do Some Animals Lay Eggs and Others Don't?

Scientists believe that the reason may be due to survival. A bird cannot carry the weight of baby birds inside it and still fly. If the bird had to fly away quickly, it would simply be too heavy.

Birds lay eggs because they can leave the eggs hidden in a safe place, while the mother looks for food or hides from predators.

An animal that runs can carry a baby inside and still move along the ground to safety. Many ground animals have long legs to get them out of danger quickly.

Did you know?
The egg of hummingbird is the size of a jelly bean, while an ostrich egg can weigh more than 3 pounds!

Why Is There No Water In The Desert?

Deserts like the Sahara can get less than an inch of rainfall in a whole year! Deserts form because the mountains along the edges prevent most clouds from reaching the area to provide rain. When rain does reach the desert, the ground is so hard it can't absorb the water and the area remains dry.

Life in the desert is so extreme, plants and animals have learned to adapt in order to survive. Plants, called succulents, store water in their stems to survive drought. Animals sleep during the intense heat of the day and only come out at night to hunt for food.

Did you know?
Camels are famous travelers of the desert, and can go for a whole week without water. They can drink up 30 gallons of water in under 15 minutes!

Why Does Ice Float?

When ice freezes, it actually gets bigger! That's because the tiny pieces that make up the liquid get very organized and spread out to take up more space. When ice is in liquid form, the pieces push together tightly and fit into a smaller area.

The strange thing about ice is that although it gets bigger, it weighs less than the same amount of liquid! Because it is so much lighter, it floats on the surface above the heavy water.

Did you know?

When ice freezes over a lake in the winter, only the top layer becomes ice. The bottom part of the lake stays liquid, so the fish and animals in the water can still swim around underneath!

How Do Icicles Form?

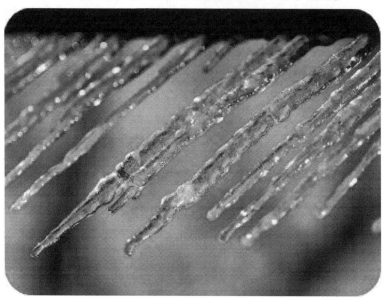

Icicles are one of Mother Nature's most breathtaking designs!

Icicles form from snow and ice melting off surfaces such as buildings or trees. As the sunlight begins to warm ice and snowfall, water drips down the edges of the surface. The cold air refreezes the water as it drops off the edge, creating a column of ice, and a beautiful icicle is born!

Did you know?
Caves have icicle-like formations called "stalactites." But stalactites aren't made of ice, they are made from a form of rock called limestone.

How Do Clouds Float?

Have you ever wanted to reach out and touch a cloud? A big cloud looks like soft, fluffy cotton. But clouds are actually made up of water droplets and ice crystals. Clouds weigh quite a bit, but they manage to stay up in the air. How do they do that?

The cloud's weight is spread out over a very large area. The water droplets and ice crystals are very tiny. Warm air that rises from the Earth pushes up the cloud and is strong enough to hold the cloud up and keep it afloat.

Did you know?
Clouds look dark and gray when they get thick with water droplets and ice crystals because the light can't shine through. They can also look grayer when close to other clouds. The clouds cast shadows on each other, sharing their dark mood.

A note to you, Dear Reader:

If this book put a smile on your face, consider putting a smile on mine by leaving a review on Amazon.com under this book's page.

I appreciate your feedback and each and every review helps me <u>tremendously</u> in improving future books so that I can provide you with a great experience.

Sincerely,
Jem

Photo Credits

I would like to express my gratitude for the following photographers, whose work illustrates my book. Their work can be found on flickr.com under their respective names.

Lightening - Steve Arnold
Snow - Alexey Kljatov
Sand - Eric Bryan
Waves - Rud Glazn
Leaves - JustyCinMD
Continents - Nicolas Raymond
Volcano - Rodolfo Araiza G.
Tornado - Recuerdos de Pandora
Diamond - Paul Hocksenar
Ocean - Christopher
Sky - James
Grass - fihu
Earth - Stephen Thomas
Seasons - andrew prickett
Earthquake - Martin Luff
Water - Ramesh Rasaiyan
Underwater - Rafae|
Lightening 2 - Daniel Palmer
Wind - Sony200boy
Monkeys - Vlasta Juricek
Earth 2 - Jason Bachman
Watermelon - Harsha K R
Air - Karrie Nodalo
Seashells - Moyan Brenn
Chicken - Ian Britton
Flowers - Riccardo Cuppini
Butterflies - John Fowler
North Pole - Jonathan Pio
Coral - USFWS - Pacific Region
Lake - Steve Cyr
Global Warming - Kevin Dooley
Rain - Gertrud K.
Animals – restructuregirl
Mountain – blemiers2
Earth 3 – ken fager
Eggs - boughtbooks
Desert - Moyan Brenn
Ice - Marko Kivelä
Icicles - Philip Chapman-Bell
Clouds - theaucitron

26272100R00028

Made in the USA
Middletown, DE
26 November 2015